LIVING WITH YOU

Other works by Barbara Blatner

The Still Position, NYQ Books (2010)
No Star Shines Sharper, Baker's Plays (1991)
The Pope in Space, Intertext Press (1986)

LIVING WITH YOU

Barbara Blatner

N̶Q̶Y Books™

The New York Quarterly Foundation, Inc.
New York, New York

NYQ Books™ is an imprint of The New York Quarterly Foundation, Inc.

The New York Quarterly Foundation, Inc.
P. O. Box 2015
Old Chelsea Station
New York, NY 10113

www.nyqbooks.org

First Edition

Set in New Baskerville

Layout and Design by Raymond P. Hammond

Cover art: Untitled, 36 x 52 inches, oil on board
© 1994 Lesley Eringer

Author photo © 2010 Lesley Eringer | www.neoimages.com

Library of Congress Control Number: 2011932516

ISBN: 978-1-935520-37-5

LIVING WITH YOU

Acknowledgements

LIFT MAGAZINE, 1992
[words give us justice]
[how do I?]
measure

SOJOURNER, 2001
that October
[time backward]

SHAMPOO, Issue 15 (online), 2002
sexual politics

BIG SCREAM, 2002
where we speak
over the top

HOUSE ORGAN, 2003
spring again

SKIDROW PENTHOUSE, 2006
[words give us justice]
[flowers and birds]

HAZMAT, 2007
[on the verge]

RED MOUNTAIN REVIEW, 2007
suddenly November

BROKEN BRIDGE, 2007
branches

HOUSE ORGAN, 2008
early evening highway

This book is dedicated to my husband
Arthur Dutton.

Contents

3 LIVING WITH YOU

4 TIME BACKWARD

ix

1

SOUND COMES INTO THE YARD

BLOSSOM

prepare
  prepare

then one day
  a word birth

and you are closer
  where
you worship:

  white-shivering bushes
leaving petals
  to the ground, phrasings
from a book—

  such is
beauty
   given.

everything
has its relationship
   to the sun

lilacs burn
  to golden curls
but their leaves stay green
  all summer

a tiny fly on my hand
is acetylene blue
    apocalyptic

across the city
  a million lives
build against
light's collateral

    for an instant,
what price
  against it all?

riches are all around—
  but justice,
where does it
  come out?

I wish it were justice enough
  this beauty.

  words
bear us
  or take us apart

I would like to know you better
I would like to know you
I would like to make
  justice with you

YARD WORK

rupturing in the yard:

  bushes   birdsong
neighbor's radio dialed
  to a news event.

  in one sector
a small pine
  is lit by sun
and in that glowing place
  a bee wanders.

my hands are full of time
  and it's only morning.

fragile the wind
    shaking the leaf
  to dapple
the porch frame

and shimmy
    grass blades'
  sensual
music all over
    the place.

my hands
touch the lilac as it palsies
        in the wind and after
when it's still.

                I sketch what I see
        onto the page
with words, falling

in the gap between
        what is true
and the words.

something deeper I'm not
        hearing...

then two birds nattering

        and a crow
toward the ledge of a tall apartment building
                swings
        her caw high

                and alights

[WHEN I WAKE THESE DAYS]

when I wake these days
   the sun is there
amazing constancy

it speaks to the yard—
   grass coming in like a meadow
twigs and branches swelling

and you with me every day
   incredible

more of the world
             speaks.

   when I push you away
I know it hurts
   but I leave to take
            my breath

I hate your silence too
   can't breathe, it's
        smoke inhalation.

these are our constant
   fluctuations

double-folded
    syntax

embedded with birds
  and voices

in this life
  with you
a grammar unfolding

SPRING AGAIN

the future pulls back, the past
        drags forward,

the present is a gash
    lilacs swing
between the poles.

if loneliness
    goes

what will you lose?

I don't know the name
    of it is
written in my body.

I face you in the past
    and the future
between two phases
    I face you.

between leaves' plaintext
    among purple blossoms
        brightness
                whittles away the extra

PARALYSIS

to be devoted
is my temptation

for lilacs have cracked into
   space again

I'd kneel in the grass before them
   but I'm self-conscious
     I hold back

two impulses happening
   at once
breaks the metric
         oh   spring

      the ecstasy of forms
winks at me
   day and night

the black blood of winter's
   come fresh and
green again

   and my vision
      always late
double-folded
        is to open it

EVERYWHERE BETWEEN US

sun surrounds us

   our bodies foretell
vast structures
     and plans

ruptures mended
  coming apart
again

sun
  moon
    cut of stars

the city
in the sun, so many words
   broken there,
glass and plastic
   scavenged
      nothing not
       returned

even the city's deathliness
  grows
beautiful in sunlight.

what we have spoken
to drowning
  hear it
     sounding

ALPHA

to find you again
  how it felt
silence and language
  holding together

the whole city
  doing it,
getting spoken,
      to air

    planes and automobiles
streak sentences
    across sky and highway
our eyes turn
        to the sound.

in the yard
  bushes' glitter
in late spring,
  a season
within the season,

is almost the last
  in an outrageous
    cycle of growth,
      complex

as cities are complex
with politics, histories,

what we can't see
   whole
streams
   towards a center
and back

while the center itself
   goes unwatched

[ON THE VERGE—]

on the verge—
there's still time—

    that's
where I want you.

    mist rises from the bushes,
ribbons of grass bind
    my toes, skies flow
over my head.

below,
    the city, multi-passionate
in all particulars
    is laid out.

last night in our closeness
    words were spoken.
the rest was up to you

    you kissed
my nipple, a deep draught
    you pulled me
        out

the city lay below
  grey
    pinnacles
      cresting,

its silence drew us together
  your mouth
    was one of its
      doors

BRANCHES

first we answer the call:

sun rising
  blazing
    melon.

    robin hopping
branch to branch
  every branch calls
    "quickly!"

irrelevant
  understanding

this light between
  branches that changes
and changes

as I change
  why shouldn't I

trust it

why shouldn't I
face myself?

face the
   sun and minister
     sky

ghost
  between
runged
  branches.

code there is
  upon the spring ground
    signals from a distance

music from someplace
  becoming
    unhidden

DAY TO DAY

look closely
  you see

pieces of
  mystery

crueler and grander
  than you'd believe

  patterned in words
   and bodies

the world grown quiet
  for the music
of another level

where green leaves curl
  their edges
from the sun.

on every side
  countries bargain
for independence

  words come together
violently

retreat and come again
    closer to where
        they try

border words
    along two edges
words at the gate

INHALATION

breath
garnered compacted
essential

energy's shroud
ready to bursting
and not—

how do I measure it?
never not in motion

your breath
against the length of mine.

rose, lilac and bee
each shroud to uncover
a rental
broken.

green rain-darkness
where we wander
breath
gathers

[WORDS GIVE US JUSTICE]

words give us justice
justice gives us words
language is that hunger

what is between us
what balance between our eyes
we fortify with kisses.

   today
lilac blossoms
  are dark gold nuggets
    speaking a late
      syntax

  the baby pine is flecked
with petals from the bush
  spreading over it

a bee travels,
  sound
comes into
  the yard

these moments as gentle
  as you touch
my face

your soft eyes
    open before and after
    the dimness

words like flesh
  knit
    or fall
        have their own breath

the cats roam in the
  leaves, investigating
      the same
over and over

  so we come back
to the old
  the new

  like the cats
in circle of

2

WHERE WE SPEAK

SUMMER COUNTRY

where midsummer sun paces
  trees fields,
the pitch of buzz
  thrums higher

and sun traces
  a just light
    on stone

and the impossible, as
  always,
is about to happen.

what do we go on?

  singed
    phrases
      burnt
          braveries—

sun
  on stone.

  we approach
each other
  confessing

your hands
　your mouth
　　your day secrets—

now is the time

　tell me

JULY

soft as sun
presses
and withdraws
from glass

meaning comes
and fades
away

heaves slow
or
cataclysmic

imparts
radiance
in either phase.

I dust worry
from your forehead

in my motion

a score
of words

a sheaf
flashing

all possibility
    wrought
  in letters

we turn
    one way
        or the other

each passage
  each
    text

MIDSUMMER SHEAVES

There is a language without speech. —Rilke

green settled, sky
   completely
  unrolled, written
    past.

lilacs long rusted
  their beauty
underground.

breeze lifts a branch,
  loosens petal
to ground—

  flux visible
    only in these
      small places

otherwise,
a groove for a while

where we fall
  toward moments
in the crux
  unseen.

what can we want
  when every cry
is hidden in a past
  season?

how can we say
  "this is not what we want"?

when what we get
  is a glimpse
of a scheme:

blue sky
  green trees
    green leaves

HIKING THE MOUNTAIN

poppy's rage
  of color
torches the wind—

what presentiment
  of intensities

  personal
and collective?

  mottoes
where we live
  and pass,

solitary passes
  where we meet
and stand
  in the silence

then slip away
   ashamed
  down the mountain.

oh the lonesome passes,
  waysides
in mountains
  torched
    with that red flower

   tokened up again
that earthly beauty

like our voices
  when we go
unashamed

    your voice
at the
  edge of itself

  passionate
to flower

[WHERE WE SPEAK]

where we speak
  words are the first thing
what takes two

  in the isolation
of the planet
  its myriad
cold and glitter,

where we speak
  pushing words
forward and back

what do we speak
  that takes two
and begins before
  and after

that the first time
  we speak
is every time?

  as in the ocean,
two white-lipped breakers:

one is thrown back
  on the other
    entirely

SUNDAY AT MOM'S

ripe flowers
     nests
  weeds

in the driveway,
  infinite
    scribbling
      cicadas

proliferate summer
  on fire

  where stalks
join other parts
  and rear
the flower

and sun
  shines
the apple dullness

possible to be filled with joy
  and soaking
    in quiet.

     how did we
come this far
     and still

so much
       is possible?

sumac
    candling crimsom
       blossoms,

eyes
meeting by chance

     but never
             by accident

INSIDE

what we have together
  comes fast
then disappears
  for a life of weeks—

not death but loss
of freedom.

a beige moth
  stammers
on the screen,

a cardinal wheels
  through
the yard

  I'm like the grey cat
waiting for sun by the window
  she is looking out.

lilacs ivory
  will shrivel to
gold rubble

language will rise
but there are many
  syllables
bound down

not to death
but loss of freedom

SHADOW ON GRASS

hot sun
speaks a solitary tongue

singes
our tropic bodies
down.

summer ranges
and we wonder
how we lived
in the old ways

but for our losses:
cocoon that never
hatches,
dark bundle,

hanging
darkness spun
round with light

it will fall
unopened
and you will look at it
with me

and you will forget it
  with me

because there is nothing else
  to do

MIRACLE WIND

days passing days
  sky unbottled
           blue

cloud
    passing from sight

the week's intense heat
   dismantled
taken apart by wind.

   birdsong blows,
grass blades ride
   the radiance,

   sun's
steadied light,

city
   skyline visible
         as sculpture again

and wind the maker
   of this new syntax

lifts my eyes
  from the floor

eyes that reach for you

TWO STORIES

yesterday
sun and wind and
   ocean
flinted around me

silver
in my eyes and hair

and I thought
I'll never get enough of this, I want
   to live
a hundred and fifty years.

in that time
I figure I could get in
   all I wanted—people,
animals, music—
   I could really live.

the sea fell back
   surf raveled
over the firm sand
   of the beach,

the light
   of five o'clock
passed from one cloud
   to another

and as I walked
  I found
an old
  innocence.

today's
a different story:

  dry house, bellowing
city, dull
  voices
      inside me.

nonetheless

  I still want
a hundred and fifty
      years

TWO IN SEPTEMBER

1.

hurricane
  coming

  wind whips
wires and bushes,

late summer peepers
  trill
morning to twilight

air is filled
with a luminous
    destruction.

    round and round
  inside the house
we move through each other

we wait
  for its breaking,

  and today
Gorbachev is ousted by coup in Russia
  and under house arrest
in the Crimea—

worlds
coming to climax

threatening
  to page apart
what's been plotted.

soon the whorl will be passing
  overhead

and we will look through
  destruction
for another figure

another cloud
  where another
    angel
      emerges

2.

another angel emerges: sun
   roams out to filament
      fierce underbelly
         of cloud.

   we peel tape
from windows untouched
   by the hurricane that never hit
         yesterday
      after all.

   this morning
the Soviet coup
   is over
the perpetrators fleeing
   "to a small Asian country,"

   crowds celebrate
in the square,

change unlit
   until the future
looking back
   brings to bear

new leaves of the rubber plant
   from freckled nubs
I didn't notice

reddish spears
   unfurl
      in the opening

BEYOND AUGUST

I'm dying
always.   why not
   get close to
as many people
   as I can?

what else might this
   life between deaths
measure to

other than
   touch, no impulse
of love
   renounced.

November's dark shield
   raises
silver air
   fine-hammered

   love gathered
and the gathering
   held

   within
its white
   numbers

REMBRANDT'S DRAWINGS

  raw morning
tree swings in wind
  rough traffic!
scream the tires

how many radial turns
  suffer these
    transmigrations,
to what
    stations?

summer suddenly
  departed

  replacing green
  with mountains of
    red and orange

you touch me
  as you've
touched me
  so many times before
    it's now and always

it's form
  and
abstraction—

life insists
   on this
      doubleness

like Rembrandt's sketches
   of canals, cottages and trees—
step close
      they're just squiggles—

step back,
   they're canals
                  cottages
                        trees.

I move fingertips
down the buttons
   of your spine

and the tree branch
   swings round

SUDDENLY NOVEMBER

this winter light seeps
    uninflected
where autumn
    radiated
        fire

and flared
    and sputtered
into its own
    energy

this light
    lends only a part
of itself
    to leafless branches
dim with ice,

sun's eternal
    flame
holds distant

    no dead flame
but in deadened state

spun larva-like
    in the clouds

a gauzed radiance
for miles

its power past breaking,

and we the numbered
  walk
under the retracted
      light

with change working
  its white sheets
    over us

for we too are bound up
  in birth

holding a fierce
  light inside

3
LIVING WITH YOU

THAT OCTOBER

rhythms
tore me
   peacefully
I started

at a threshold
   opening devotions

I knew we were for
   each other
that warm fall night
   walking toward my house,
darkness writing
   without a word—

a little jump
in the solar plexus—
   we both felt it

no word
but a syllable—

so I was timed for you

and spaces everywhere
      between.

the statistician blinds herself
  with braille
the poet goes out
  on a limb
the lawyer palpates
  loss and intention
the word is
  waterfall between

I turn to you for the
    flare

[WHERE WE DARE]

where we dare to love
words come then sift away

oceans flare
along the coast
their gleam wakes us.

words brighten
or obscure,
their funding
is transitory

a paragraph takes shape
in the wilds,
catches on trees, wires,
   depends
            on earthly things

so I depend on you

the lore of your voice mouth hands

where I dare
   to move

BURNING BOOK

I forget I'm alone
  it's shocking
I can open your arms
  I can get to them

there was no reason to love you
  it was an accident.

time turns
  toward us
    and away

wars keep happening
  three hundred thousand
    reckon
      the quarrel
      of two

the world grows smaller
  conflict ignites
from closeness, like
  the burnings
    of childhood

all those accidents

and
resuscitations—

and now
    to find a way through

BED

words

are not the first thing

they are
to speak

something
comes through
  their mask.

I touch your face your lips
I move
    to touch

your ass your balls
    I reach
toward what will make me
  as human as you

where words
are not the first thing

the monsterous angelic
  parts of ourselves
    come together

my moistness
  your hardness
each ringed with a wand
  of rough-sweet hair

after this
  we rise

and come down
                    after

we rise

          after

               we come

down

words are the first
  things
we speak

73

OVER THE TOP

"there's nothing
more temporal than orgasm"
        I say

and you laugh—
and nothing's
        more temporal than your
                        laughter

except all seasons
  light
withers,

    light:
  great pooled
betrayer signifier
    saviour.

why can't I ride you
  longer?

  but everything
moves quick to a crest
  exactly
and over.

now fossil night
  rises
toward us,

  now
you rest—

but
  ready again,
        when?

ripe rose vagina
  and
pink cock sticking-up

    ready and wet again
to make time?

BEFORE SLEEP

where we started
  was confused
and still

light rattles there
more freely now

fierce light and a splendor
  of confusion
sticks us
  in paradise,

your back to me
  in bed
my arm
  across your waist,
    so *home.*

    "my punishment was to be happy"
said Neruda.
  boy are we foolish

all voices
  and signals
    go unpunctuated

where words trail to
  silence
no disturbance is as fine
  as words

SEXUAL POLITICS

sun tosses
in the burning leaves

the ozone is a burning book

we're around each other

last night when we fucked
   I got angry
I liked it so much

leave me alone

my body's a politic
   I want it.

across the sky, dead lilacs
   shiver golden lava

   I think
we are close
   seeking a language
but is it true?

the U.S. has
so many languages, we
   have many
within our own ranged words, wordless dictionaries
   nothing settled

except you rode me, bucking bronco,
   to the skies and back

ANGRY WORDS

mallets

blunt challenges
between them

and I don't even know
where the anger was
what it came from

more percussion
than meaning

but from that
sound, hard new syntax
takes over.

a single orange lily
trumpets
off the trellis
in the garden.

another music
this anger
another notation

DYING WORDS

thrum of the refrigerator

you turn in bed.

    outside the window
a bush ignites
  in blossom.

from the kitchen table
from a great distance
  I watch you.

sometimes I want to be
  free of our bond
I can't say why
  words aren't
    those places

  and I am afraid
for the beginning
  of those
    words

love comes hard
  scarcely entering
the language

DUST ON THE FLOOR

repartee
between words
where I watch you
come from a weight

weightier than
words

or thought,
mingling
with an absent light,

watch your eyelashes click
against your dark eyes

you're still
a boy
face puckish and sharp,

also a man
angular in the cheekbone

and in words
yes in words
you were long a man

before you turned
  back into a boy

and I saw you
clearly
  through silence

which is its own
    medium
  leaded like ocean

your legs
  prance it high

before
  it knocks you
    over

COME AGAIN

how I touch and lose you
  is the same

as we sleep
  all violence disentangles

so I don't remember
  what it would be like
not to have you

  though it's only been
three years
  under the same covers

same dust
  same moon
in the morning sky

white scale
  absolute in
its traces.

now leaves turn
  blood and copper's
bright decay

like words decay
out of meaning
   into new reams

as one touch
reckons
   another

[HOW DO I]

how do I
  get closer to you
and not fall under?

I write you with my mouth
  shoulders and hands
    the paragraph is numberless

dark text lies between the stars,
  planets churn to gloss,
shadows lay down on branches
  every sophisticated instrument
evolves to
        out-of-focus

the consciousness of this room
  bares
time to us

your breath enumerates you

chains of forgetting, silver-
  worded with spaces between,
    lay across me

I come to you forgetting

in order to come back
       I forget

LIVING WITH YOU

plants grow in the dark
time with you is between

I turn to the clock
you pull me back

how many times
have you pulled me back?

the first time
in your old apartment
you didn't let me leave.

   morning is still a strain
to separate
   from sleep
from each other

   to rise
checkered with shadow
   toward
the fearful symmetries

oh but we are learning to face
   them

from coiled
   words of dark
      to pronounce
   between them
         to cross

and not draw back

decked with shadow
we move between
      two worlds

4
TIME BACKWARD

[TIME BACKWARD]

time backward
the clock released

in shadow waits all shadow
the morning principle

moves us towards night
and round again
to morning

unmeasured
except for

minutes folding back
ridges in leaves.

words have taken us this far
  but there are ways
    other than words—

an ant laboring a spot
  of food across the pavement—
action more precise
  than the finest paragraph—

carries what needs
to be carried

EARLY EVENING HIGHWAY

look at the moon
  look

heavy moon
  more than full

fruitless
  on lavender sky

six o'clock
  birds subdued

moon weightless
  clanging

  washed
  pendant
compassionate
thoughtless moon

I would take you

out of the sky
  you are heavy

such an open
  syllable
hanging over us all

  even in ghostly remission
on the world's
  other side,

moon belonging
  to everyone and
everyone
  to this moon

  and no return from it
not the longing
  or the image
brushed on the sky

this scar
  we travel by

DAY OF THE DEAD

rain speaks all day
  sharpens
goes smaller

  larger,
hollows
    is burnished.

umbrellas parade
    overground.

this lapse of sun
  brings
no sorrow
  but its consistency

notating
  all over
the ground

wind groaning
through it all

and finally
  in intervals
it all comes down

loosening rags
letting fall
  every bone of sky

our dead
  all the dead

pour down

MEASURE

I hold on to you
away from the world,
try to find strength to go
there again

no matter what happens

the oceanic world
rocks around us
to us
broken glass, sky
on water, mixing elements,
tragic switching shapes.

closer are objects
we know by ourselves—
a shoe on the rug
a blue candle
their silence is a clock

its minutes
interleaved

move us
forward and back

AT THE ZOO

out of nothing
  comes something:

peacock standing
     below a concrete bridge
  in the globed aviary
at the zoo

in slow-mo,
     sprays open
his tail, feather by
     feather

  separates the deck

and weighted there
  by his great
turkey tail

he screams

and a little boy
  on the bridge
leans over

   and screams.

the small birds squall
  upwards
from the

    catastrophe, light on whatever
  rock or branch
they can—

alarm in the wake of such
        noise and
magnificence

    that seems
to break in
  from another world

but it's this
  world
the massive edge

he unfolds
  in his voice
and tail

[TONIGHT]

tonight
    the smallness

of my
    life

    against
death's
    genius

comforts me
    I surrender

at kitchen
    table
to my activity:

digging words
    with pen
onto paper

while you
    sound bottle
against
    butter dish

deep
   in refrigerator,
swig from
   bottle, smack

lips, a tiny
  joyful
noise,
   hum

   piece
of song.

I look up,
  amazed

at your
   human
      sound

RELIGION

window-light presses
  our white-paper shade:
faint traces of the saints

transparency
  pressing toward us
extra light

look to it, it's common
  in nature
always

the radiance unpeeling
  what is not
essential,

unsacrificial, a great
  reasonableness
untempered by disdain
  or praise

ADIRONDACK

river through an opening—

where?

canoe
   slipping laketide
by the big pine

trees part
    reveal
  the channel
invisible

     till we get
right next to it

    as the river
curves and curve
  takes over

and our boat
   hovers
above a clear
    sandy bottom.

look!

a heron appears
  in that cavity
where your thoughts
  are not

grey-sapphire
  flapping over the water

voluptuous
    flying

under gloom and gold
  resurrecting
a cloud's

    satchel ecstasies

[FLOWERS AND BIRDS]

flowers and birds
collude in beauty
  uninstructed

through the clock
the great rounding
  delivers us

  language is fragments
we pick up
  we turn
      over and again

the soul or whatever you call it
  in words
looks hard from its traces

  I look to your eyes
for retrieval
  and get back the light of
a smile

  for you too
collude in beauty
  an edge where we go

only to and no more

the light
I fiddle
　from your eyes

where we do not
　　go
everything is waiting

About the Author

Barbara Blatner is a poet, playwright and composer-musician. She lives in northern Manhattan with her husband and two cats, and teaches in the English Department at Yeshiva University. *The Still Position, a verse memoir of my mother's death*, was published by NYQ Books in 2010. *The Pope in Space*, a poetry chapbook, was published by Intertext Press (1984). Barbara's verse play *No Star Shines Sharper* was published by Baker's Plays (1991), produced for radio and aired repeatedly on National Public Radio stations. Her plays have been produced in New York, Boston and Cleveland. She has written musical scores for theatre, including the Boston Shakespeare Company and New Theatre, and songs for the Boston-based fusion group Urban Myth with whom she played keyboards for five years.

About NYQ Books™

NYQ Books™ was established in 2009 as an imprint of The New York Quarterly Foundation, Inc. Its mission is to augment the *New York Quarterly* poetry magazine by providing an additional venue for poets already published in the magazine. A lifelong dream of NYQ's founding editor, William Packard, NYQ Books™ has been made possible by both growing foundation support and new technology that was not available during William Packard's lifetime. We are proud to present these books to you and hope that you will continue to support The New York Quarterly Foundation, Inc. and our poets and that you will enjoy these other titles from NYQ Books™:

Barbara Blatner	*The Still Position*
Amanda J. Bradley	*Hints and Allegations*
rd coleman	*beach tracks*
Joanna Crispi	*Soldier in the Grass*
Ira Joe Fisher	*Songs from an Earlier Century*
Sanford Fraser	*Tourist*
Tony Gloeggler	*The Last Lie*
Ted Jonathan	*Bones & Jokes*
Richard Kostelanetz	*Recircuits*
Iris Lee	*Urban Bird Life*
Linda Lerner	*Takes Guts and Years Sometimes*
Gordon Massman	*0.174*
Michael Montlack	*Cool Limbo*
Kevin Pilkington	*In the Eyes of a Dog*
Jim Reese	*ghost on 3rd*
F. D. Reeve	*The Puzzle Master and Other Poems*
Jackie Sheeler	*Earthquake Came to Harlem*
Jayne Lyn Stahl	*Riding with Destiny*
Shelley Stenhouse	*Impunity*
Tim Suermondt	*Just Beautiful*
Douglas Treem	*Everything so Seriously*
Oren Wagner	*Voluptuous Gloom*
Joe Weil	*The Plumber's Apprentice*
Pui Ying Wong	*Yellow Plum Season*
Fred Yannantuono	*A Boilermaker for the Lady*
Grace Zabriskie	*Poems*

Please visit our website for these and other titles:

www.nyqbooks.org

www.ingramcontent.com/pod-product-compliance
Lightning Source LLC
LaVergne TN
LVHW011426080426
835512LV00005B/295